STEM IN CURRENT EVENTS

▸ Agriculture ▾ **Energy** ▸ Entertainment Industry ▸ Environment & Sustainability
▸ Forensics ▸ Information Technology ▸ Medicine and Health Care
▸ Space Science ▸ Transportation ▸ War and the Military

ENERGY

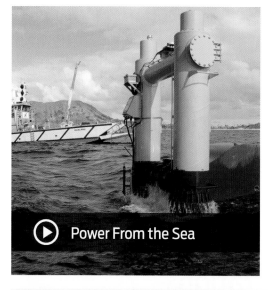

▶ Power From the Sea

▶ Smart E-Meters

▶ Wind Turbine Tech

ENERGY

By Michael Burgan

MASON CREST

Mason Crest
450 Parkway Drive, Suite D
Broomall, PA 19008
www.masoncrest.com

© 2017 by Mason Crest, an imprint of National Highlights, Inc.

Printed and bound in the United States of America.

First printing
9 8 7 6 5 4 3 2 1

Series ISBN: 978-1-4222-3587-4
ISBN: 978-1-4222-3589-8
ebook ISBN: 978-1-4222-8290-8

Produced by Shoreline Publishing Group
Designer: Tom Carling, Carling Design Inc.
Production: Sandy Gordon
www.shorelinepublishing.com

Front cover: Northwest Energy Innovations/Department of Energy (top left); Wikimedia (top right); Allouphoto/Dreamstime (bottom)

Library of Congress Cataloging-in-Publication Data

Names: Burgan, Michael.
Title: Energy / by Michael Burgan.
Description: Broomall, PA : Mason Crest, [2017] | Series: STEM in current events | Includes index.
Identifiers: LCCN 2016004733| ISBN 9781422235898 (hardback) | ISBN   9781422235874 (series) | ISBN
    9781422282908 (ebook)
Subjects: LCSH: Energy industries--Juvenile literature. | Biomass energy--Juvenile literature. | Renewable energy
    sources--Juvenile   literature.
Classification: LCC TJ163.23 .B87 2017 | DDC 621.042--dc23
LC record available at http://lccn.loc.gov/2016004733

Contents

Key Icons to Look For

 Words to Understand: These words with their easy-to-understand definitions will increase the reader's understanding of the text, while building vocabulary skills.

 Sidebars: This boxed material within the main text allows readers to build knowledge, gain insights, explore possibilities, and broaden their perspectives by weaving together additional information to provide realistic and holistic perspectives.

 Educational Videos: Readers can view videos by scanning our QR codes, providing them with additional educational content to supplement the text. Examples include news coverage, moments in history, speeches, iconic sports moments, and much more!

 Text-Dependent Questions: These questions send the reader back to the text for more careful attention to the evidence presented here.

 Research Projects: Readers are pointed toward areas of further inquiry connected to each chapter. Suggestions are provided for projects that encourage deeper research and analysis.

 Series Glossary of Key Terms: This back-of-the-book glossary contains terminology used throughout this series. Words found here increase the reader's ability to read and comprehend higher-level books and articles in this field.

INTRODUCTION
Finding Energy

When cold weather comes, you're probably able to make yourself comfortable indoors by turning up the thermostat. Within seconds, the furnace kicks into action, burning a fuel such as natural gas or heating oil. Energy stored in the atoms of the fuel is released and turned into heat, which soon reaches you and takes the bite off that cold day.

Energy exists in different forms all around us, and for hundreds of thousands of years, humans and their ancestors have sought to use that energy to make life easier for themselves. Energy provides warmth, fuel for cooking, and electricity to power our smartphones and other gadgets. Energy also propels vehicles, from scooters to mammoth ships to spacecraft that explore the planets. Modern life as we know it would not be possible if humans hadn't discover ways to convert the energy all around them into forms that they can use.

One of the first great human inventions was making controlled fires to provide heat, cook food, and keep away dangerous animals. Fires occur naturally, of course, as when lightning strikes spark forest fires. Even heat from the sun can cause a wildfire. But building controlled fires, with grasses and then wood for fuel, led to great improvements for people.

Energy from the sun (solar power) was another natural force humans learned to use to their advantage. They positioned their homes so that in winter they could get as much heat from the sun as possible. Animals were also a source of energy, whether used to pull a cart or turn the wheels of mill that ground wheat into grain.

The energy sources of today's world can be more complex, thanks to the developments made in the STEM fields over the last several hundred years. During the 19th century, the creation of an engine powered by burning gasoline, and the discovery of vast amounts of petroleum, led to the dominance of the car as a source of transportation. Today, more than one billion cars travel the world's streets, along with trucks, buses, and other vehicles. Splitting the atoms of certain elements to release the energy stored inside is the source of nuclear power, which was first used to create electricity for homes in 1955.

Scientists also discovered and harnessed forms of energy that we couldn't see, but that are all around us. Inside every atom are charges of electricity. Discovering how the positive and negative charges interact led to the creation of generators that create the electricity that power our appliances, as well as batteries that let us take electrical power almost anywhere we want to go.

Discovering new energy sources and how to convert them into usable forms has undeniably made life easier for most of us. But that process has also created problems that humans are wrestling with today. Many of the fuels used to power vehicles or heat homes create pollution that harm the environment. Removing the fuels from the ground can also be damaging. Mining coal on Earth's surface, for example, can lead to the destruction of trees or the polluting of nearby waters.

Burning coal and petroleum also contribute to global warming. The planet's temperature has always varied over time. But starting in the mid-20th century, scientists saw a rise in the amount of carbon dioxide in Earth's atmosphere. This gas is a byproduct of burning coal, oil, and other resources to create energy. The rise of carbon dioxide and other harmful gases produced by energy production are linked to rising temperatures that most scientists believe threaten the planet's overall health. The evidence today comes in various forms, including melting glaciers and more intense heat waves than ones in the past.

Today, the men and women in STEM fields that deal with energy face several important issues. Can they find new sources of energy that won't harm the planet, but are also affordable? Can they make older forms of energy more efficient? Can they build networks that reliably send electricity where it's needed as demand for it rises? Around the world, scientists and engineers of different backgrounds are trying to answer these questions. At times, their fields overlap. Here's a look at just some of the promising developments in the STEM field that could solve the world's energy concerns.

The growing use of solar panels for energy shows how science, technology, and engineering are combining to change the way that we find the power we need for our homes and businesses.

SCIENCE AND
Energy

Words to Understand

consumption   the act of using a product, such as electricity

electrodes   materials, often metal, that carry electrical current into or out of a nonmetallic substance

inorganic   describing materials that do not contain the element carbon

nuclear   referring to the nucleus, or center, of an atom; or the energy that can be produced by splitting or joining together atoms

organic   describing materials or life forms that contain the element carbon; all living things on Earth are organic

reactor   a device used to carry out a controlled process that creates nuclear energy

Making energy involves a wide range of scientific disciplines. Many energy researchers have a background in one or more of the branches of physics or chemistry, for example. Biologists also play a role in looking for new fuel sources. Meanwhile, scientists who study the human mind and behaviors seek ways to understand why people do what they do when it comes to how they use—or waste—energy. The scientists often work closely with people who take basic scientific ideas and use them to create new technologies or energy systems. In this chapter, we'll look at recent scientific theories and projects related to energy production and **consumption**.

Creating the Sun's Energy on Earth

When we look up at the sun, we see a simple yellow orb. But in the core of the sun and other stars like it, a powerful process is constantly producing tremendous amounts of heat, with temperatures reaching 27 million degrees Fahrenheit. The source of that energy is a process physicists call **nuclear** fusion.

The Energy of Nuclear Weapons

The process of splitting atoms to release energy is called nuclear fission. It was used to create the powerful bombs that the United States dropped on Japan in 1945, just before the end of World War II. Later, even more powerful nuclear weapons called hydrogen bombs used the fission process to create an immense amount of heat to trigger the fusion process. In the weapon, the process is uncontrolled. Making fusion energy that can create electricity or perhaps power a vessel requires a great deal of control over the temperatures created. Only a tiny amount of fuel is heated to high temperatures at any one time, and not enough to cause an explosion.

Inside the sun, atoms of hydrogen collide with each other and fuse, or join, together. As a result, the hydrogen atoms produce helium while also releasing energy. In one second, the hydrogen inside the sun produces 600 million tons of helium, along with huge amounts of energy. During the 1930s and 1940s, scientists began to understand nuclear fusion and to look for ways to create fusion energy on Earth. The focus soon became to use the energy as a source of power for electricity. Fusion would be "clean," not producing the harmful gases that come from burning coal, and it would generate electricity more consistently than sun or wind power can.

The University of Washington's "dynomak" project is trying to create a much smaller and safer reactor as a new way of generating electricity.

Creating an affordable fusion **reactor**, however, has proven difficult. A typical coal-fired electric power plant is much cheaper to build than a fusion reactor that can generate the same amount of electricity. But in 2014, scientists at the University of Washington announced that they had a design for a fusion reactor that was more affordable. Leading the team was physicist Thomas Jarboe, an expert in plasma, the fourth state of matter (along with solids, liquids, and gases). Plasma is created when energy is added to a substance, releasing electrically charged particles called electrons from atoms.

Working from the design of an existing fusion reactor, Jarboe and other scientists created what they call a dynomak. Fusion reactors rely on magnetic fields to heat plasma inside a chamber and keep the fusion process going. These fields are typically created by large coils outside the reactor. In the dynomak, electrical current goes directly into the plasma to create the magnetic fields, resulting in a simpler and cheaper reactor.

Jarboe and his team created their design for a reactor about one-tenth the size of one that would be used to create electricity for consumers. They hope to increase the size of their test models

Dr. Thomas Jarboe led the team that created this model of a dynomak, which uses plasma to help generate electricity much more quickly and cheaply.

to prove that the dynomak will safely and efficiently produce energy, at a cheaper cost than a coal-fired plant. "Right now," Jarboe said in a University of Washington press release, "this design has the greatest potential of producing economical fusion power of any current concept."

Building Better Solar Panels

The idea of collecting energy from the sun to create electricity isn't new. In 1839, a young French scientist named Edmond Becquerel exposed certain metal **electrodes** to light and created small amounts of electricity. The substances absorbed the light and then released electrons, which can be captured to create an electric current. Becquerel's discovery was later called the photovoltaic or photoelectric effect—"photo" referring to light.

Today's solar panels are made up of individual units called photovoltaic cells, which typically use silicon to capture sunlight and convert it to electricity. But as with the materials Becquerel used in the 19th century, silicon is not completely efficient at turning all the sun's energy into electricity. The cells used in the typical home solar panel might be able to convert just 15 percent or so of the energy into a usable form. Scientists, though, think a new kind of material can make solar cells that are more efficient and cheaper than current photovoltaic cells. The new cells are made from materials called hybrid perovskites.

In experiments in the lab, scientists learned that perovskites that contained a halide compound (halogen mixed with one of a number of different elements) had photoelectric properties.

The mineral perovskite

Solar cells made from perovskite are transparent, but also thin and flexible. Scientists hope that there might be a newer and safer way to make the popular energy product.

Further work showed that mixing **organic** and **inorganic** compounds increased that ability to turn light into electricity. Since 2006, scientists have created different hybrid perovskites, seeking to improve their ability to make that conversion. Today, some perovskite solar cells have a 20 percent efficiency. That might not seem like much, but it's 25 percent more than earlier cells.

Some recent research focused on understanding how the hybrid perovskites work. Scientists at the University of Texas and the University of Utah have found a way to test different perovskites to see which ones will work best in generating electricity. They use magnetic fields, which detect the activity of electrons in the photovoltaic material. Understanding the physics of the perovskites will make it easier for scientists to improve their performance in solar cells.

Scientists are also experimenting with how to make perovskite solar panels safer to make and more affordable. The first perovskite cells contained lead, a substance that can be harmful to humans. Lead poisoning can cause joint and muscle pain, headaches, and high blood pressure, among other symptoms. In extreme cases, it can be deadly. In 2014, scientists at the Argonne-Northwestern Solar Energy Research Center in Illinois and at the University of Oxford independently discovered that they could replace the inorganic lead with another inorganic but safer element—tin. Their first tests showed the tin cells had about 5 percent efficiency, but both teams expected to increase that quickly. The independent and almost simultaneous discovery on two continents showed the worldwide interest in perovskite cells.

The future is here—renewable energy sources.

Another breakthrough in producing the cells came in 2015, as scientists at Brown

University in Rhode Island announced they had found a way to make thin films of the cells. Previous methods to make the films required high heat—more than 212 degrees Fahrenheit—and the process sometimes reduced the cells' efficiency. The new method allows the films to be made at room temperature and at lower costs. The films are thin enough for some light to pass through. Some day soon, different colored films of the perovskite cells could be used as energy-producing window decorations.

Biofuels for the Future

One energy source used to replace gasoline is biofuels, a term that covers fuels made from plants or some waste products, such as used cooking oils. One crop commonly grown for biofuel is corn, but other plants show more promise. They can not only provide fuel but also help farmers who grow a mix of food crops and energy crops. That's the conclusion scientists working for the Department of Energy came to in 2015 after work they did on a test farm.

Not all fields produce the same amount of crops. A cornfield, for example, might have areas that have less nitrogen in the soil. That chemical is commonly used as a fertilizer, and too little of it means less corn grows. But too much nitrogen leads to the creation of nitrous oxide, a gas even more harmful than carbon dioxide when it comes to creating climate change. A form of nitrogen called nitrate also tends to run off the soil and pollute rivers. Christina Negri, a soil and plant scientist, led the research to see how the biofuel plants switchgrass and willows could control the use of nitrogen and help farmers to still make money.

Corn is just one of the many biological products that scientists are finding can be a source of energy beyond its original use as food.

Switchgrass and willows have deeper roots than corn. They can take nitrogen out of the soil that corn plants can't reach. Planting them in areas where nitrogen levels are low means farmers don't have to add more nitrogen to produce a crop they can sell, as they do when they try to grow corn there. The farmers save money on fertilizer while producing a biofuel crop they can also sell. Negri told Phys.org that her goal was to convince farmers that they and the environment could benefit by this targeted analysis of the soil and planting of the biofuel crops. "We wanted to show that it's doable," she said. "If we design for specific outcomes, we'll see real results." The goal is to eventually do this kind of mixed farming on a much larger scale.

Energy and Sciences of the Mind

If you turn down your thermostat on a winter night, do you really save energy? After all, won't it take more energy to get the house back up to a comfortable temperature in the morning?

Actually, no. Yet some people cling to that myth and to patterns of behavior that can waste energy in the home, on the road—or on the battlefield.

In the quest to use fewer kinds of fuel that contribute to global warming, psychologists and behavioral scientists are trying to learn what people think and do when it comes to their energy use. The scientists' goal is to change long-held thoughts and frequently performed actions so consumers will reduce their energy consumption.

In the United States, the largest user of energy in various forms is the military. In 2013, its energy bill cost taxpayers almost $19 billion. All branches of the military are seeking ways to change old habits to save fuel. That way soldiers, sailors, and Marines won't simply rely on new technologies that improve fuel consumption.

For the Marines, one issue was how long some trucks are kept idling before being driven. Older models of some trucks required the idling. Even though newer versions didn't, Marines who had used the old ones kept up the old habits. An experiment used special gas gauges on some of the trucks, so a unit's drivers could see how much fuel they saved if they idled less. Another unit didn't have the gauges, but the ones that did quickly saw that their gas consumption went down because of the reduced idling. Seeing concrete results from their changes made it easier for them to accept the new procedures.

The Navy is also looking to cut down on fuel consumption by its planes and ships. Elke Weber, a psychologist working with the Navy, said changing the software used to buy equipment could be one step in cutting fuel consumption. Humans often

Using a bit of pyschology and technology, the Navy and the Marines are helping to save taxpayer dollars and energy by changing how their vehicles are fueled.

A key to energy use in the future will be to continue to convince people to use renewable sources and to recycle. Can psychologists find ways to change people's minds?

have what is called a status quo bias—they are more likely to keep doing what they have always done rather than embrace change. So, when buying equipment, Navy personnel might automatically want to buy what they've used before, even if it's not fuel efficient. But specially designed software could generate a recommendation for certain needs that automatically suggests the most fuel-efficient option.

Weber said overcoming people's habits is important for consumers' energy choices, too. An electric company, for example, might send customers a card saying they can check a box to choose to have a cleaner power source for their home electricity. But consumers are not likely to change what they already have. More energy savings would come if the company simply switched everyone to the cleaner source and told customers who didn't want to switch that they had to mail in a card saying so.

Making changes in behavior is important, Weber argued, because human behavior will shape how quickly people make needed changes in energy policies and production. She told the *Washington Post* in 2015, "Behavioral science...tells you how to implement all of these other solutions in a different way."

 ## Text-Dependent Questions

1. What is the process that harnesses the sun's energy and could one day be used to create electricity on Earth?

2. What does the photoelectric effect refer to and how does it relate to energy production?

3. What are the benefits of planting switchgrass in fields where nitrogen levels are low?

 ## Research Project

Using sources found on the Internet, determine which U.S. state produces the most electricity from solar power.

Electric cars are not new; several companies make all-electric or hybrid models. What is new is the way that batteries are changing to be longer-lasting, cheaper, and more effective.

TECHNOLOGY AND
Energy

2

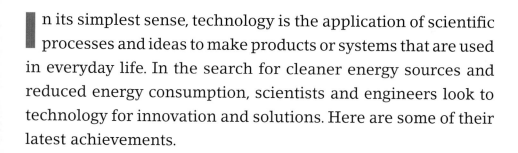

Words to Understand

evaporate   to change from a liquid to a gas

ion   an atom or molecule containing an uneven number of electrons and protons, giving a substance either a positive or a negative charge

microorganisms   tiny living creatures visible only under a microscope

sustainable   able to be used without being completely used up, such as sunlight as an energy source

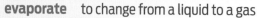
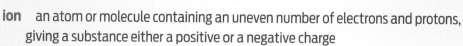

In its simplest sense, technology is the application of scientific processes and ideas to make products or systems that are used in everyday life. In the search for cleaner energy sources and reduced energy consumption, scientists and engineers look to technology for innovation and solutions. Here are some of their latest achievements.

Building Better Batteries

From electric cars to computers of various sizes, batteries are an important power source. Here's a look at three recent developments in the effort to build better batteries.

• Many of today's batteries are built around lithium, the lightest known metal. One disadvantage, though, is that a lithium-**ion** battery can lose its ability to fully recharge fairly quickly—even if it's not used. And if a lithium-ion battery is damaged, it can explode. A better solution, scientists at Stanford University say, is the aluminum-ion battery they demonstrated in 2015. Aluminum is cheaper and safer than lithium, and a battery made from it can recharge in a minute and work longer than existing rechargeable batteries. An aluminum battery, however, is much heavier than a lithium one that produces the same amount of energy. Right now, that weight difference limits how aluminum batteries can be used. One possible use is to regulate the flow of electricity through power lines. The battery could store extra energy in the system, then quickly release it when demand for electricity rises.

• Since lithium-ion batteries won't be replaced any time soon, scientists are looking for ways to improve them or the process for making them. Scientists at the Massachusetts Institute of Technology (MIT) have designed a new lithium battery that is much cheaper to make. A typical lithium battery has many layers of electrodes, which move the battery's electrical current to the device it's powering. The new batteries have fewer but thicker electrodes, and so are easier to produce, making them cheaper as well. The new battery, its creators say, can also be bent or folded and still operate, making them safer than today's lithium-ion batteries.

• Batteries work by converting the energy in certain chemicals into electricity. Then they need electricity to recharge the chemicals so they can create electricity again. A new battery, though, could end the chore of plugging in a battery-operated device to recharge it. Scientists in India have developed a battery that recharges with artificial light, with no solar cell required. The simple version of the battery that has been tested can power a small fan and then recharge in 30 seconds while exposed to indoor light. The battery is safer than lithium and other batteries, and cheaper to recharge. The scientists will have to improve its performance to make it useful in commercial products.

Lithium-ion batteries power dozens of devices in our homes and offices. Scientists are not satisfied with how they work, however, and are looking at improved models.

Plant-e technology holds out the promise of using the power generated by living plants to create electricity that can be harnessed.

Power Phones With Plants?

When farmers look out over their fields, they see a crop that will provide money for their family and feed many people. When Dutch scientists looked out over similar fields, they saw a form of energy waiting to be harvested.

Starting in 2007, scientists at Wageningen University began exploring how to tap the energy plants produce as they grow. Now, the Dutch company Plant-e is using that knowledge to make products that use plant-generated electricity to power lights or provide energy to recharge a cell phone.

The new technology rests on how plants grow. Plants take energy from the sun in a process called photosynthesis. That energy helps the plants produce their own food. Actually, the plants produce more food than they need, and the extra material goes back into the soil in which they grow. Then, **microorganisms** in the soil eat this extra food. During that process, the organisms release electrons. The Plant-e products use a device made from carbon to collect the electrons and create electricity.

Scientist and Plant-e cofounder Marjolein Helder said that taking the electricity from the soil is safe: "We don't need to damage the plant, it's a noninvasive system." And as long as the water in the soil does not freeze or completely **evaporate**, the energy can be removed 24 hours a day. Adding more water or letting the ice melt can restart the collection process if it does stop. Comparing plant power to other **sustainable** forms of energy, such as solar and wind, Helder thinks her product has clear advantages. "This system works at night and when there's no wind," she said.

Plant-e's current system is a roughly 33 feet-by-33 feet (10-by-10 meters) square filled with plastic containers for the plants and electrodes that collect the electricity from the soil. A system that size can provide power to a wi-fi connection source or LED lights. The technology can be made even more efficient, Plant-e makers believe, so

Tapping into plant energy to charge phones.

that within a few years the same-sized system could provide most of the electricity for an average Dutch family.

Japan's Microgrids

While most electrical grids are large, after a 2011 earthquake and tsunami hit parts of Japan, some companies decided they were better off connecting to smaller grids. The shutdown of larger grids during the natural disaster left the companies without power for several weeks. Now, some Japanese companies are building microgrids, small smart grids that provide power for just one or a small group of factories. In 2013, Toyota started a microgrid that uses both natural gas and solar to create electricity for seven factories in one region. Honda has been doing something similar for new homes built outside Tokyo. A Honda manager says the microgrids now define "smart" electricity production for Japan. Naohiro Maeda told *IEEE Spectrum*, "Our goal is to produce the energy on-site that we need to consume on-site." For homes, that means using solar panels to produce electricity, batteries to store it, and a small gas-fired system that creates heat for hot water and some electricity.

Plant-e sees some of the greatest potential for its product in remote parts of Asia, where rice is commonly grown. The water in the rice paddies is plentiful and never freezes, so plant power could provide electricity to regions that currently don't have it. Plant-e is still developing collection tubes that can be placed in the paddies or other watery areas where plants grow.

Smart Meters at Home

For the companies that provide electricity to homes and businesses, all the talk today is about the smart grid. The grid refers to the entire system used to generate and transmit electricity from the power plant where it's created to the end point where it's consumed. The smart grid uses computers and sensors that transmit information about the flow of electricity to make sure the entire system works as it should.

Devices called smart meters are an important part of this high-tech grid.

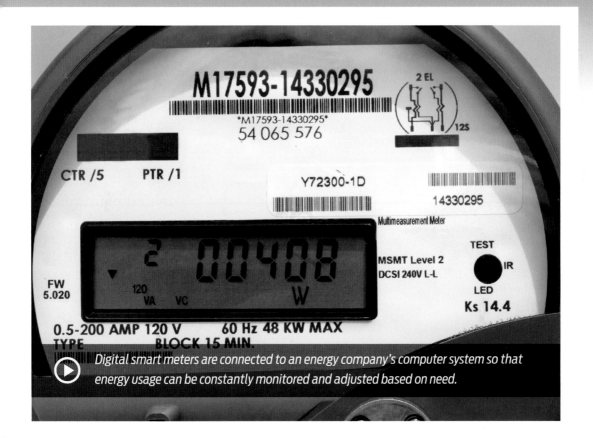

Digital smart meters are connected to an energy company's computer system so that energy usage can be constantly monitored and adjusted based on need.

Electric companies install them at homes and businesses to record how much electricity is used and when. Millions have been installed since 2007, with more added every year. Experts expect the United States to have 132 million smart meters installed by 2020.

In a typical home, the meters record energy usage every hour, then send the information over a wireless network to the power company. The meters can tell a company when the power might have been cut off. They also provide information that companies

Smart Grid Technology offers optimal control of power systems.

The installation of smart meters is spreading across the country, as more and more cities and towns see the long-term benefits of this technology.

can share with consumers. The goal is to encourage people to shift more of their energy consumption to times of the day when the overall demand on the grid is low. That shift makes it easier for power companies to provide enough electricity when it's most needed. Some companies charge cheaper rates when the demand is lower, which helps convince customers to use more electricity at those times and less when demand and prices are high.

In the future, the use of smart meters to help consumers use electricity more wisely could mean power companies have to build fewer generation plants, which typically burn fossil fuels. Electric companies also save fuel since they don't have to send out workers to read each meter, as they did in the past.

Text-Dependent Questions

1. Which kind of rechargeable battery is cheaper to make and safer to use: one made with lithium or one made with aluminum?

2. What is the advantage of producing energy from the soil in which plants grow compared to using solar or wind power?

3. What are microgrids, and where are they currently being used?

 Research Project

Search the Department of Energy website to find three ways in which the U.S. government is promoting the development of smart grids.

Before the science of solar power can be turned to use, engineers and builders have to create collection points for the energy from the sun, such as this array of panels in New Mexico.

ENGINEERING AND
Energy

Words to Understand

fossil fuels   fuels in the earth that formed long ago from dead plants and animals

piston   part of an engine that moves up and down in a tube; its motion causes other parts to move

prototype   the first model of a device used for testing; it serves as a design for future models or a finished product

radiation   a form of energy found in nature that, in large quantities, can be harmful to living things

turbines   an engine with large blades that turn as liquids or gases pass over them

L ike technology, engineering involves taking scientific ideas and turning them into practical uses. Engineering, though, often does this on a large scale. Instead of making a small device to extend a battery's life, engineers might create a huge device for improving the collection of solar energy, as is going on in New Mexico. But as with the other STEM fields, engineers and their projects can overlap with science, technology, and math. Here are some recent engineering efforts to improve how we create and use energy.

A curved, fish-eye lens was used to show the full height of the Sandia Labs' Falling Particle Receiver, an experimental power-generating machine.

More Energy From the Sun

With plenty of sunshine year round, the high desert of New Mexico is the perfect place to experiment with new ways of collecting more solar energy. And that's what engineers at Sandia National Laboratory have been doing, as they test the Falling Particle Receiver. The receiver was first installed in 2015 at the top of a 200-foot tower at the National Solar Thermal Test Facility's lab. The tower, the only one of its kind in the United States, lets engineers collect data to see how they can build plants that generate sun-fueled electricity on a large scale.

The Falling Particle Receiver may have the ability to make it cheaper to generate that power. It circulates tiny bits of ceramic through the solar tower, which focuses sunlight into a powerful beam. The light heats up the ceramic "sand," which is then stored in insulated tanks. Their heat can then be used to boil water to create steam, which powers electrical generators.

Similar processes using a form of salt soak up and store the sun's energy, but the salt begins to melt above 1,100°F (593°C). The Sandia engineers hope the ceramic particles will work at up to 1,800°F (982°C). The increase in temperature means more energy is available for creating electricity, which will reduce the costs.

An Unseen Energy Source

If you spill some water, eventually it will dry up in a process called evaporation. Evaporation uses heat in the air to turn water or another liquid into a gas or vapor. "Evaporation is a fundamental force of nature," Columbia University professor Ozgur Sahin told Science Daily. "It's everywhere, and it's more powerful than other forces like wind and waves."

Realizing the power of evaporation, Sahin and a team of researchers made a tiny car that is powered by the evaporation of water. Another device they created is a tiny engine that floats in water and uses evaporation to power a light.

The key to the first evaporation-powered vehicle is an engine called the "Moisture Mill." Crucial to that engine's operation are living organisms called spores. Sahin had earlier learned that changes in humidity can make a collection of the spores expand and contract. He put the spores on strips of tape, and the movement of the spores made the tape move like a flexing muscle.

Sahin and researcher Xi Chen placed the spores on the tape in a case with shutters that opened and closed. When water in the case evaporated, the spores expanded, which opened the shutter and let the humidity in the case escape. That then made the spores contract, which closed the shutters and let humidity build up again. Thanks to the spores, the changes in humidity were repeated over and over. The system acted like a **piston** in an engine, which became the heart of their Moisture Mill engine. Sahin then attached the engine to a tiny car, which ran on evaporation power. The engine also powered a generator creating electricity that made a small light bulb flash.

Sahin thinks a full-sized Moisture Mill could some day sit above a large body of water and use evaporation to produce large amounts of energy to generate electricity. The work with evaporation could also lead to cars that don't require fuel or batteries to run.

More Water Power

Water is at the heart of two engineering projects trying to create more sustainable energy. The movement of water, whether the constant motion of the ocean's waves or a river funneled through a dam, creates energy that can be used to generate electricity.

By moving up and down with both waves and tides, this device, called "Azura," can generate electricity in almost any weather.

The U.S. government has been looking for ways to harness wave energy, and in 2015 it began testing a wave energy converter (WEC) off the island of Oahu.

The device, called Azura, weighs 45 tons and stands upright in the water. As the waves move around it, it turns the energy in the waves into electricity. Azura is the first WEC in the United States to be connected to a power grid and have its use verified by an independent institution—in this case, the University of Hawaii.

What makes Azura special is how it collects the energy. Waves move both side to side and up and down. Unlike most WECs, Azura can capture the energy in both sets of wave movements.

To reach this point, the company that built Azura first had to test its design indoors, in a wave tank. Then it built a **prototype** that was tested off the coast of Oregon in 2014. Azura was tested in Hawaii for a year, so engineers could find ways to improve its performance and build more WECs that they can connect to the grid.

A power company in Oregon created a way to turn the energy from moving water in Portland's pipes into electrical energy for consumer use.

Unlike Hawaii, not every place has access to ocean waves, or even a river. But every city has drinking water flowing through publicly owned pipes. And that water could be another source of electricity. Lucid Energy, a company in Portland, Oregon, has designed a system that taps the energy that water creates as it flows through the pipes from a high location to a lower one. Portland's water flows down to the city from sources near Mount Hood. Some of the city's water pipes now contain **turbines** connected to generators that turn the movement of the water into electricity. Pipes outside the city are wide enough to hold the turbines, but some day smaller turbines could go into the narrower pipes that feed homes and businesses. In 2015, the system created enough electricity for 150 Portland homes. And unlike dams built to create electricity from rushing rivers, the new system does not threaten wildlife.

Solar-Powered Flight

Using solar panels to power an airplane is not new, as model aircraft used energy from the sun during the 1970s, and a pilot first flew a larger solar-powered plane in 1980. Since then, advances in engineering led to a record-setting solar-powered flight in 2015, part of an effort to make the first flight around the world in a solar plane.

Pilot and designer Andre Borschberg of Switzerland flew the *Solar Impulse 2* from Japan to Hawaii without stopping, setting a record for the longest solar-powered flight, measured by both distance and time in the air. The 4,482-mile (7,213-km) trip took just under five days. What made it possible for the *Solar Impulse 2*

Einstein and Energy

In their search to create energy from sources besides **fossil fuels**, today's scientists and engineers can pay tribute to the brilliant Albert Einstein. In 1905, the German-born Swiss scientist wrote a paper explaining how sunlight can, under certain conditions, create electricity. While Edmond Becquerel had earlier discovered this photoelectric effect, he did not know why it happened. In 1921, Einstein won one of science's top honors, the Nobel Prize in Physics, for his idea. Einstein also came up with the famous formula $E=mc^2$, which means energy equals the mass of object times a constant number—the speed of light—multiplied by itself. The equation helps explain the amount of energy that can be created during nuclear fission, and it shows that mass itself is a form of energy. The energy inside an atom of uranium or other materials is released during the fission process. In 1939, Einstein saw the potential to use nuclear fission to produce energy, which could be used to create a bomb. He urged the U.S. government to conduct more research on fission, especially for a bomb, before the country's enemies did.

to fly nonstop were the batteries it carried to store the sun's energy. The batteries recharged during the day so the plane could keep flying at night.

Additional design features made the *Solar Impulse 2* different from other planes as well. It needed large wings to hold solar panels, yet it needed to be as light as possible so it would use the least amount of energy. Borschberg and a team of 50 engineers and technicians used carbon fiber, a light but strong material, and built a wingspan of 237 feet (72 m)—longer than the wings on most passenger airplanes. Yet *Solar Impulse 2* weighs just under 5,000 pounds (2,267 kg), about the same as an average car.

Another challenge was how to keep Borschberg and a second pilot, Bertrand Piccard, safe on long flights. Once over the Pacific or another ocean, they would not have a chance to land for days. But to keep the plane light, the cockpit had to be relatively small, while still holding food and other supplies. The pilots spend their time in a seat that reclines—and

The *Solar Impulse 2 airplane weighs only as much as a standard car, but can fly for thousands of miles using only energy from the sun.*

also serves as a toilet! Waste goes into bags that are dropped out of the plane as it flies.

The Pacific crossing burned out batteries on board *Solar Impulse 2*, but Borschberg planned to fix them and continue his and Piccard's quest to circle the world using solar power. The trip was meant to show the value of "clean" technologies that don't pollute the planet.

Smaller May Be Better

Engineers built the first nuclear reactors to create electricity during the 1950s. Today, large reactors use fission to produce power around the world. But building these power plants is expensive. It can also be difficult to build them in remote areas. In recent years, companies around the world have been working on different designs for small modular reactors (SMRs). They can be built in a factory and trucked to a site in small pieces called modules, then assembled. Engineers, though, are working to make sure SMRs are safe. Any nuclear power plant runs the risk of an accident that could release deadly radiation.

While U.S. companies are still working on their SMR designs, a Russian company owned by the government has already built and tested small reactors that sit on barges. The reactors can be brought by sea to areas near Russia's Arctic region where mining is going on. The distance from developed areas and the extreme climate would make it expensive to build a full-sized nuclear reactor or other kind of power plant. The SMR can provide both heat and electricity. Another Russian-designed SMR is being developed to power icebreakers. These specially designed ships keep ice out of the sea lanes used by other ships in cold waters.

In the United States, the company Babcock & Wilcox (B&W) received money from the government in 2012 to develop a land-based SMR. The company can transport the modules to a site by truck, ship, or train. More reactors can be added later if energy demands increase. B&W says its SMRs will help fill the growing demand for electricity in the United States, while also replacing older power plants that are no longer efficient to run.

From Waste to Energy

Each year, climbers seeking to scale Mount Everest leave behind a lot of garbage—and tons of their own waste. Local workers have to carry that waste from the base camps at Everest and other nearby mountains to the village of Gorak Shep, which is at an

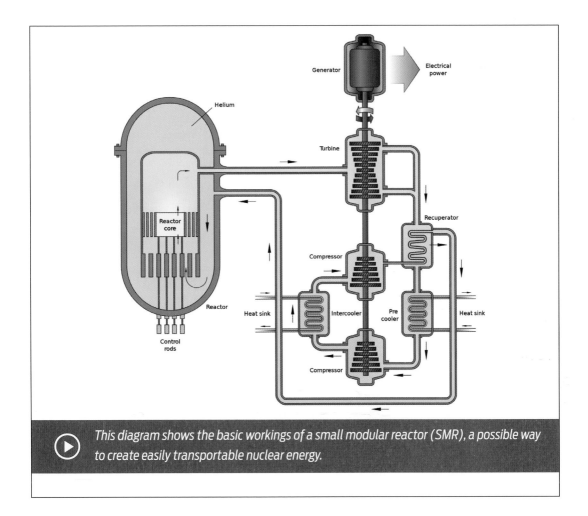

This diagram shows the basic workings of a small modular reactor (SMR), a possible way to create easily transportable nuclear energy.

elevation of almost 17,000 feet (5.18 km). The waste goes into large outdoor pits, where it slowly dries. But in the meantime, it creates a mess that could threaten the local water supply.

Garry Potter, a retired U.S. engineer, and Dan Mazur, a mountain climber, teamed up to create a way to get rid of the mess and

Innovative engineers are working on a way to turn the collected trash on Himalayan mountains into energy that can help local villages.

provide energy for Gorak Shep. Their Mount Everest Biogas Project is building a plant that captures methane gas in the waste, which villagers can burn for cooking, heating, and light. Similar biogas plants are found in other parts of Asia, but building one in an isolated spot with a cold climate presented challenges. The bacteria that turn waste into gas need a fairly high constant temperature. The project engineers' solution included burying the unit in which the bacteria work and using solar panels to collect energy to power coils that heat it. Batteries store extra power to keep the entire system running on cloudy days.

Power From the Road

Electric cars aren't new—some of the first cars built in the late 19th century ran on battery power. Now, the desire to burn less fossil fuel is renewing interest in electric cars. The batteries, though, tend to be heavy and expensive and need to be recharged often. One solution may be building roads that can recharge the batteries as the cars drive, using a process called magnetic resonance coupling.

Scientists and engineers from the Korean Institute of Advanced Science and Technology began testing such a system in 2010. With the online electric vehicle (OLEV) system, an electric tram drew power from coils placed under the road at a Seoul, South Korea, zoo. Sensors in the road indicated when the tram was approaching the coils so they could begin transmitting magnetic energy. Another set of coils on the tram changed the magnetic fields into electricity that powered the vehicle. While the tram also had a battery, it was much smaller and lighter than the ones found on electric cars.

Since the first test of the OLEV system, it has been tried with buses, and in 2013 the Korean city of Gumi used OLEV buses as part of its public transportation system. Drivers of the trams and buses watch a monitor that helps them keep their vehicles lined up with the underground coils. This makes sure the vehicles draw as much electricity as possible. The creators of OLEV plan to improve the system by adding a device to the bus that automatically detects the magnetic field beneath it, so it follows the path that creates the most electricity.

In 2015, the United Kingdom announced plans to test a magnetic resonance coupling system on its roads to power electric cars. Building a complete road system with this wireless electrical system, however, will be expensive. In South Korea, putting the OLEV system under about 1.5 miles of roads at the zoo cost $550,000.

Great Gas Mileage

While the world looks to electric cars to reduce the production of carbon dioxide, the reality is that gas-powered cars will be on the roads for decades. That has led scientists and engineers to look for ways to build cars that use less gas. The engineers of tomorrow can play a role in that too, as the Supermileage Competition for college students shows.

The competition is sponsored by SAE International, a group of engineers from many different fields. The Supermileage Competition was first held in 1980, and it aims to draw attention to worldwide efforts to improve the gas mileage of vehicles. In 2015, a team of engineering students from Université Laval in Quebec, Canada, built a car that could go almost 2,100 miles on just one gallon of gas! Of course, its car and the other cars in the competition are not like the ones found in the average driveway. These cars have much smaller engines and are designed to

No batteries! OLEV trains such as this one in South Korea operate on electric coils placed in the ground. They present a new opportunity for low-energy mass transit.

Canadian university students won an international competition by creating this car that could go more than 2,000 miles on a gallon of gas.

carry only a driver. They also travel at much slower speeds than regular cars do. The Laval car averages about 19 miles per hour.

To achieve such impressive gas mileage numbers, the Laval team focused on reducing the weight of the vehicle. It and the other cars are also designed to reduce drag, a force that makes a vehicle need more power to move. The Laval students made changes to the engine, too, so they could better control the amount of gas burned.

Text-Dependent Questions

1. What source of energy relies on changes in humidity to power a tiny engine?

2. How was the *Solar Impulse 2* built so that it could use no fuel and fly at night?

3. Some of the work done by Albert Einstein influenced the research on what two forms of energy?

 Research Project

Research Lucid Energy and its water-pipe turbines in Portland, Oregon. What other locations besides Portland use, or could soon use, its system to create electricity? What are other ways that cities might use their moving water to make energy?

The power of supercomputers and networked computers is being put to use to run calculations that might help change how we use and create energy in the future.

MATH AND
Energy

Words to Understand

capacity   the amount of a substance that an object can hold or transport

congestion   an oversupply of something resulting in limited movement

intermittently   not happening in a regular or reliable way

simulations   things created on a computer to provide information about how an object or process might work in the real world

utility   a company chosen by a local government to provide an essential product, such as electricity

athematics is at the heart of much of the research that goes on in science. It's also an essential part of working out engineering problems. When it comes to reducing energy consumption or looking for new ways to produce energy, companies often turn to a branch of mathematics known as big data. It has been defined as math that looks for patterns in large amounts of data so people can do things more effectively.

The introduction of computers and, more recently, mobile apps, has made it easier for scientists and engineers to capture large amounts of data quickly and then search for those informative

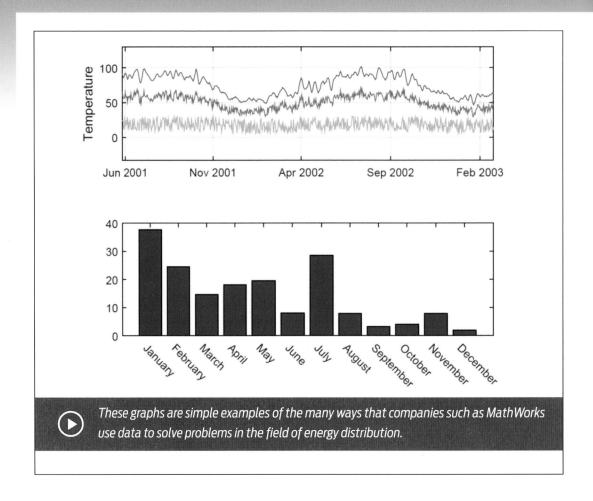

These graphs are simple examples of the many ways that companies such as MathWorks use data to solve problems in the field of energy distribution.

patterns. Here's a look at how both big data and mathematical calculations are having an impact on the energy field.

Making Math Work

What location is the best for building a new wind farm? Which areas of the ocean have more oil and gas beneath their floor than others? Can scientists pinpoint the best place to build a large-scale solar farm?

Answering these kinds of questions is important for the scientists who work for energy companies. The companies don't want to waste money drilling for oil or building solar farms that are not going to produce enough energy to cover their costs. That's where MathWorks comes in. The company, based in Massachusetts, offers software that analyzes the data companies gather before undertaking a huge project. MathWorks products can also gather data and create computer **simulations** and models of how things might work in the real world.

One "family" of software MathWorks sells has a range of features, from analyzing statistics to creating models for how efficient a particular solar panel will be. With wind farms, the software can take historical data on wind speeds in a certain location and predict how much energy might be generated there, depending on the size of the turbine. Building a wind farm as cheaply as possible also requires knowing the best way to get the power from the farm to the electrical grid. Computer models helped a Canadian power company determine the process before it built a new wind farm, saving it time and money.

Fuel Cells: the Future?

In the world of sustainable energy, fuel cells present another option. They run on a mixture of hydrogen and oxygen. Hydrogen is considered the fuel, and it can be easily obtained from water or certain organic materials. A chemical reaction between the hydrogen and oxygen creates electricity and small amounts of water. Fuel cells can provide power to lights or propel cars with an electric engine. Fuel cells can also provide backup power to factories in remote locations.

During the 1960s, NASA considered fuel cells the safest and most reliable way to provide power for the spacecraft that took the first humans to the moon. Some auto companies are now making cars powered by fuel cells, which do not create any pollution. In Japan, thousands of people are using them to power their homes.

Another company used MathWorks products to improve the production of its fuel cells. The software helped create algorithms, which are the series of instructions that tell a computer how to do a certain task. In this case, the algorithms controlled how the fuel cell operated under certain conditions and helped the company lower its costs.

A Formula for Efficiency

Generating electricity from solar and wind power is good for the planet, but it presents challenges to electric companies and the power grids. Under certain conditions, an electrical grid might not have the **capacity** to carry all the power from various generation

No matter how electricity is generated, stations such as this one are needed to spread the energy from a central point to the many homes and businesses that need it.

By spinning at a high rate in the wind, these tall turbines generate electricity with no harm to the environment and will surely be a big part of energy creation in the future.

plants to customers. When this **congestion** occurs, some of the power from renewable sources might not get fed into the system. Rather than see that energy go to waste, Binayak Banerjee and others at Australia's Curtin University created a mathematical formula to address the problem.

Power companies rate the capacity that their lines can carry based on worst-case weather conditions. Since those conditions are rarely met, the power lines are often not at full capacity. For those times when lines do get congested, companies could build a new system with more capacity. But as Banerjee told Science Network Western Australia in 2015, "build[ing] a bigger network…is time consuming and expensive and may not be economically viable as renewable sources produce high output only **intermittently**."

Banerjee's solution is tied to a concept called Dynamic Line Rating (DLR). It takes into account conditions as they happen and allows for the lines to carry more capacity. DLR requires a smart grid to work effectively. Banerjee suggested that DLR could allow power companies to briefly overload the transmission system to take in the extra energy produced by solar and wind farms, rather than keeping it out of the system. He and others at Curtin University used a formula to conduct simulations of having the momentary overloads with a DLR system that's part of a smart grid. The simulations suggest the idea can work, meaning during those times when, for example, a wind farm boosts its energy production, the power will go into the system.

The Math of Micro-Forecasting

For companies that rely on the sun and wind to create power, having the most accurate forecast available is key. IBM, the U.S. computer and software company, announced in 2013 that it had a big-data solution to the problem: a tool it calls Hybrid Renewable Energy Forecasting (HyRef). The system gathers data from a variety of sources and feeds it into supercomputers to create what are called "micro-forecasts," or weather forecasts for a specific wind or solar farm that can change every 15 minutes.

Lloyd Treinish, an IBM scientist, called himself and the other HyRef scientists "data scavengers." He told a company newsletter in 2014 that some of the data comes from weather stations run by various government agencies. But HyRef also gets information from the skies: from NASA spacecraft. "They give us a lot of detailed information about the Earth's surface—such as temperatures, land use, soil types, terrain details," Treinish said. All these factors on the surface can influence weather. So can the presence of buildings. A large number together, as in a city, can raise temperatures. HyRef calculations take into consideration the interaction between city "heat islands" and the weather. Other sources of information include cameras that track the movement of clouds and sensors on wind turbines that measure wind speed, direction, and the temperature.

Treinish said that HyRef can also help power companies prepare for storms that might damage their equipment. The system can

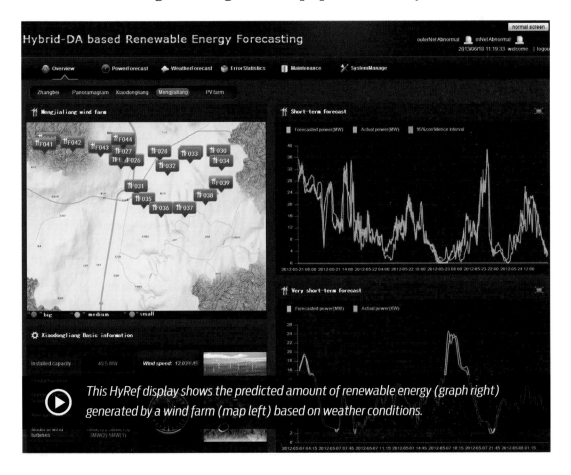

This HyRef display shows the predicted amount of renewable energy (graph right) generated by a wind farm (map left) based on weather conditions.

The electrical grid depends on hard-wired transmission systems. Mathematical models can help predict damaging storms to help get the grid up and running quickly.

tell not only where the storm will hit but the kind of destruction it might cause. With that knowledge, the companies know how many repair crews might be needed and where they should go.

The ultimate goal is to reduce the uncertainty of solar and wind energy production because of the uncertainty of the weather. Power companies want to know if they will have a consistent flow of electricity. HyRef will take out some of the uncertainty and make it easier to add solar and wind farms to the grid, rather than having to add more generation plants powered by fossil fuels.

Big Data and Consumers

While complex calculations can improve energy transmission and production, big data also has a role to play on the consumer side. Ethical Electric provides homes with electricity generated from renewable resources. Customers, though, have to choose to make the switch from their local electricity provider. Even people who are concerned about global warming and the environment might not make the effort to make that switch, since using Ethical Electric costs more each month than getting power from the local utility company. And companies that sell the green energy don't want to waste money advertising their services to people who aren't likely to make the switch.

The solution, Ethical Electric believes, is finding those customers most likely to want to get their energy from renewable sources. The way to do that is to analyze publicly available data on those people. The company reviews the information in various databases, then targets the people who would be most likely to sign up with Ethical Electric. Perhaps they have given money to groups or lawmakers who support sustainable energy. Tom Mattzie, head of the company, explained that sending out an ad to 1,000 homes at random might get only one customer to switch, which would cost the com-

Different forms of energy.

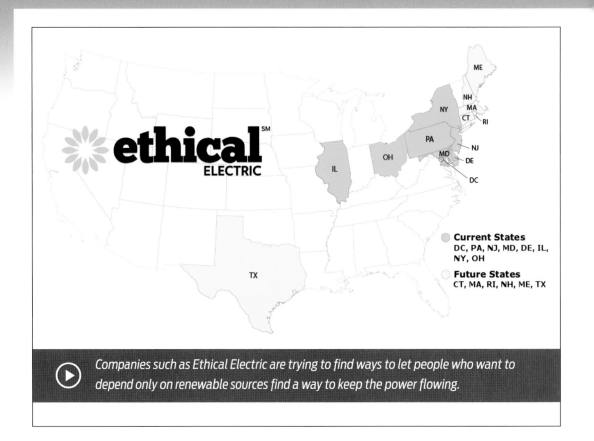

Current States
DC, PA, NJ, MD, DE, IL, NY, OH

Future States
CT, MA, RI, NH, ME, TX

Companies such as Ethical Electric are trying to find ways to let people who want to depend only on renewable sources find a way to keep the power flowing.

pany too much money; it could never succeed as a business. But, as he told *The Guardian* in 2014, "talking to sixty and getting one out of sixty is a business." Since 2012, getting customers to make the switch to Ethical Electric has kept hundreds of thousands of tons of carbon dioxide out of the atmosphere.

Calling on the skills and innovation of science, technology, engineering, and math, experts around the world are changing the face of energy. Nothing is more important to the growth of society and its people than having safe, plentiful, and dependable energy. STEM is pointing the way to the future of energy.

Text-Dependent Questions

1. How did a Canadian power company use simulation software before building a new wind farm?

2. How does Dynamic Line Rating (DLR) differ from the older method of measuring capacity on power lines?

3. What are two of the sources of information that help the HyRef system make micro-forecasts for wind and solar farms?

 Research Project

Not all states allow consumers to choose their electricity provider and so get electricity from companies like Ethical Electric. Go to the website of the American Coalition of Competitive Energy Suppliers to see if your state allows choice. If it does, what are some of the choices available? If it doesn't, search for how much of your state's power comes from sustainable sources.

Find Out More

Books

Green, Robert. *How Renewable Energy Is Changing Society*. San Diego: ReferencePoint Press, 2013.
Part of a series on science and society, this book looks at the different types of renewable energy and the pros and cons of their use.

Hillstrom, Kevin. *Nuclear Energy (Hot Topics)*. Farmington Hills, Mich.: Lucent Books, 2014.
Controversial—but potentially world-changing—nuclear energy holds both promise and peril.

Hunter, Nick. *The Race to Find Energy (World in Crisis)*. Minneapolis: Lerner, 2014.
Scientists and societies are seeking new ways to power the planet; this book examines some of the newest ways.

Websites

IEEE Spectrum: Energywise
http://spectrum.ieee.org/blog/energywise

Phys.org: Energy and Green Tech
http://phys.org/technology-news/energy-green-tech/

Popular Mechanics: Energy
http://www.popularmechanics.com/science/energy/

Science Daily: Energy Technology
http://www.sciencedaily.com/news/matter_energy/energy_technology/

Series Glossary of Key Terms

capacity the amount of a substance that an object can hold or transport

consumption the act of using a product, such as electricity

electrodes a material, often metal, that carries electrical current into or out of a nonmetallic substance

evaporate to change from a liquid to a gas

fossil fuels a fuel in the earth that formed long ago from dead plants and animals

inorganic describing materials that do not contain the element carbon

intermittently not happening in a regular or reliable way

ion an atom or molecule containing an uneven number of electrons and protons, giving a substance either a positive or negative charge

microorganism a tiny living creature visible only under a microscope

nuclear referring to the nucleus, or center, of an atom, or the energy that can be produced by splitting or joining together atoms

organic describing materials or life forms that contain the element carbon; all living things on Earth are organic

piston part of an engine that moves up and down in a tube; its motion causes other parts to move

prototype the first model of a device used for testing; it serves as a design for future models or a finished product

radiation a form of energy found in nature that, in large quantities, can be harmful to living things

reactor a device used to carry out a controlled process that creates nuclear energy

sustainable able to be used without being completely used up, such as sunlight as an energy source

turbines an engine with large blades that turn as liquids or gases pass over them

utility a company chosen by a local government to provide an essential product, such as electricity

Index

Credits

Dreamstime.com: Stefano Lunardi 8, Rawpixelimages 20, Torian Dixon 22, Anton Starikov 25, Stephen Pietzko 29, Nyker1 32, Sergiy Mashchenko 50, Mariusika11 54, Imantsu 55, Rafael Ben-ari 58; University of Washington: 11, 12; Boshu Zhang, Wong Choon Lim Glenn & Mingzhen Liu: 14; Andrew Silver/USGS: 14 inset; 350jb/DT: 17; US Navy/Lance Cpl. Christopher Rojas: 19; Plant-e/Wageningen Univ.: 26; Openei.org: 30; Randy Montoya/Sandia National Laboratories: 34; Northwest Energy Innovations/Department of Energy: 37; Sherri Kaven courtesy of Lucid Energy: 38; Solar Impulse/ABB/Anna Pizzolante: 41; Alfred Runow/ Martin Edström Photography: 44; Ahn Young-joon/AP Images: 47; Courtesy University of Laval: 48; MathWorks: 52; IBM: 57; Ethical Electric: 60.

About the Author

Michael Burgan has written more than 250 books for children and teens, many of them about science and technology. He has written biographies of Thomas Edison, George Washington Carver, and Nikola Tesla, among others, and explored such topics as making flu vaccinations, pursuing careers in genetic engineering and food science, and studying bats. A graduate of the University of Connecticut, Michael is also a playwright. He lives in Santa Fe, New Mexico, with his cat, Callie.